In PORTRAITS I look for the unguarded moment, the essential soul peeking out, experience etched on a person's face ... When I find the right person or subject, I may come back once or twice, or half a dozen times, always waiting for that right moment. Unlike the writer, once I pack my bags, there is no chance for another draft — either I have the shot or I don't. This is what drives and haunts the professional photographer, the gnawing sense that 'this is it'.

For me, the portraits in this book speak a desire for human connection; a desire so strong that people who know they will never see me again open themselves to the camera, all in the hope that at the other end someone else will be watching – someone who will laugh or suffer with them.

From an outpouring of pictures over 20 years, these are the faces I cannot forget. Some stare out of places I don't want to remember. All of them represent chance connections in a world of resilience.

*Steve McCurry*

Φ

Timbuktu, Mali, 1987

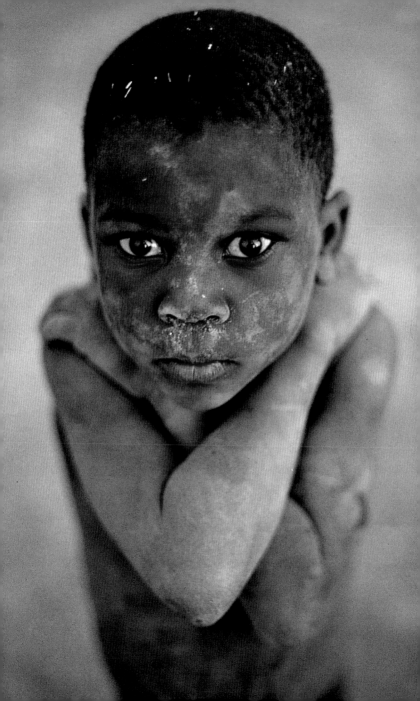

Kabul, Afghanistan, 1993

Jodhpur, India, 1997

Kashmir, India, 1995

Nuristan, Afghanistan, 1990

Kathmandu, Nepal, 1979

Lhasa, Tibet, 1989

Diré, Mali, 1986

Ladakh, India, 1996

Rangoon, Burma, 1994

Los Angeles, USA, 1991

Rajasthan, India, 1996

Ghazni, Afghanistan, 1990

Hong Kong, 1985

Tahoua, Niger, 1986

Rome, Italy, 1990

Chitral, Pakistan, 1980

Timbuktu, Mali, 1985

Basilan Island, Philippines, 1985

Porbandar, India, 1984

Bombay, India, 1994

Luzon, Philippines, 1986

Dhaka, Bangladesh, 1983

Darjeeling, India, 1994

Bamako, Mali, 1985

Beijing, China, 1989

Bali, Indonesia, 1983

Sylhet, Bangladesh, 1983

Rig-Rig, Chad, 1985

Herat, Afghanistan, 1991

Rangoon, Burma, 1995

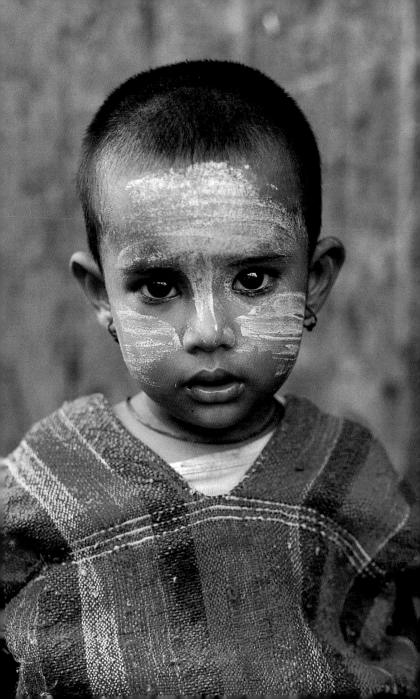

Kabul, Afghanistan, 1993

Marpha, Nepal, 1998

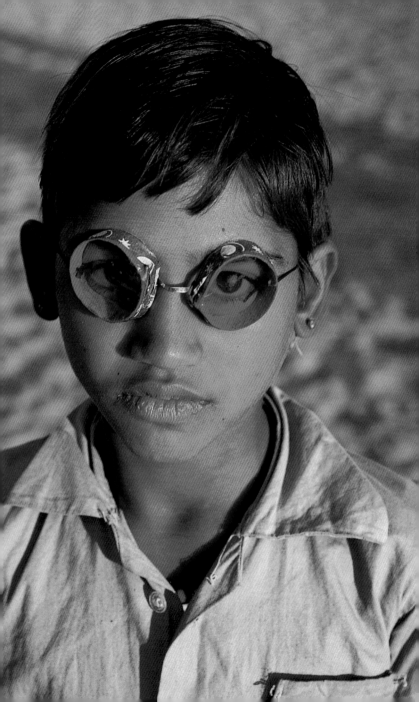

Kuala Lumpur, Malaysia, 1990

Aranyaprathet, Thailand, 1979

Haridwar, India, 1998

Baghdad, Iraq, 1986

Hong Kong, 1984

Iloilo, Philippines, 1985

Darwin, Australia, 1984

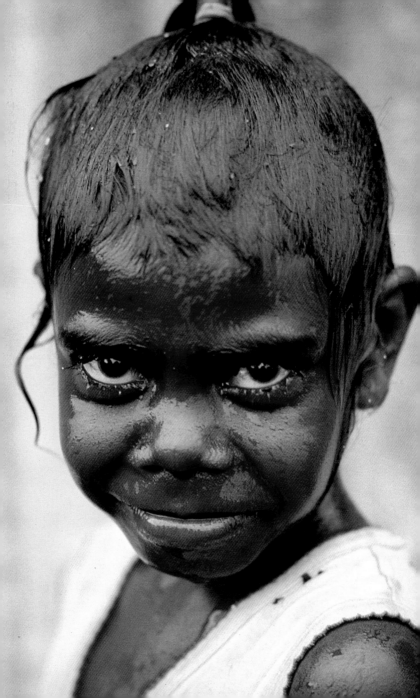

Chicago, USA, 1987

Mandalay, Burma, 1995

Ladakh, India, 1996

Banaue, Philippines, 1985

Ladakh, India, 1997

Bamian, Afghanistan, 1992

Chicago, USA, 1987

Bombay, India, 1994

Loikaw, Burma, 1995

Dharmsala, India, 1997

Porbandar, India, 1983

Gao, Mali, 1986

Herat, Afghanistan, 1991

Asmar, Afghanistan, 1979

Kandahar, Afghanistan, 1990

Herat, Afghanistan, 1992

Bombay, India, 1995

Niamey, Niger, 1987

Marseilles, France, 1989

Rangoon, Burma, 1995

Banaue, Philippines, 1985

Baluchistan, Pakistan, 1981

Kabul, Afghanistan, 1988

Insein, Burma, 1984

Aranyaprathet, Thailand, 1980

Marseilles, France, 1989

Haridwar, India, 1998

Iloilo, Philippines, 1985

Ladakh, India, 1996

Khartoum, Sudan, 1985

Kandahar, Afghanistan, 1990

Kosovo, Yugoslavia, 1989

Jaipur, India, 1982

Jabal os Siraj, Afghanistan, 1992

Kabul, Afghanistan, 1993

Tibet, 1989

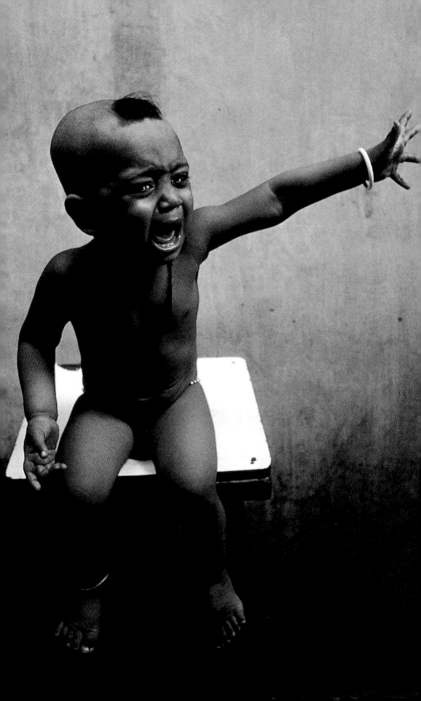

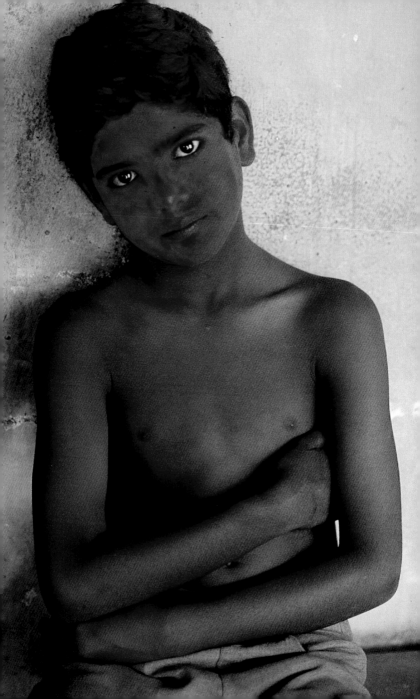

Baluchistan, Pakistan, 1980

Manila, Philippines, 1985

Los Angeles, USA, 1991

Los Angeles, USA, 1991

Los Angeles, USA, 1991

Ladakh, India, 1997

Lhasa, Tibet, 1989

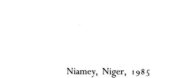

Niamey, Niger, 1985

Filadelfia, Paraguay, 1985

Zamboanga, Philippines, 1985

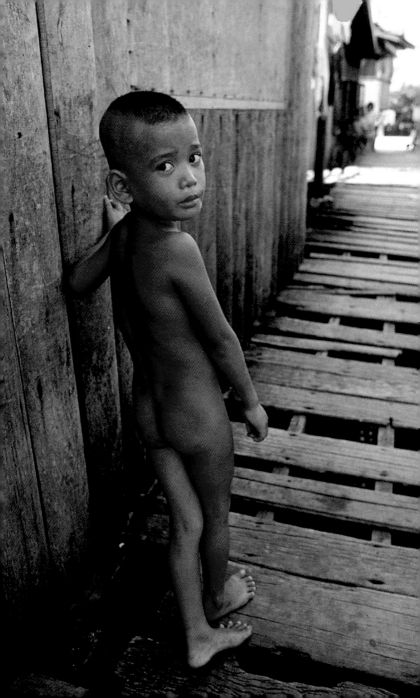

Gao, Mali, 1986

Charikar, Afghanistan, 1990

Los Angeles, USA, 1990

Kuala Lumpur, Malaysia, 1989

Ladakh, India, 1978

New York City, USA, 1994

Kabul, Afghanistan, 1991

Haridwar, India, 1998

Rangoon, Burma, 1995

Amritsar, India, 1996

Amritsar, India, 1996

Los Angeles, USA, 1992

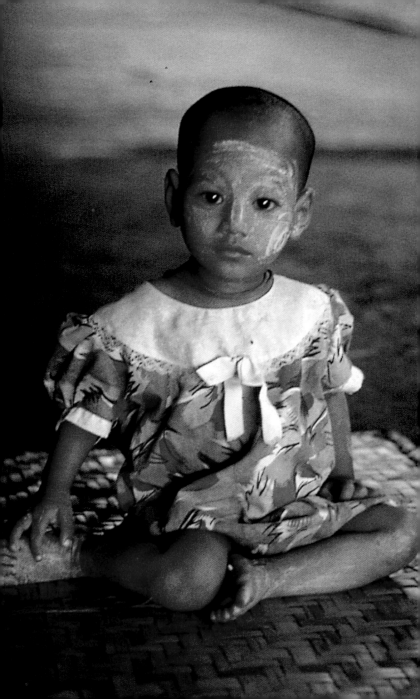

Kabul, Afghanistan, 1992

Mopti, Mali, 1986

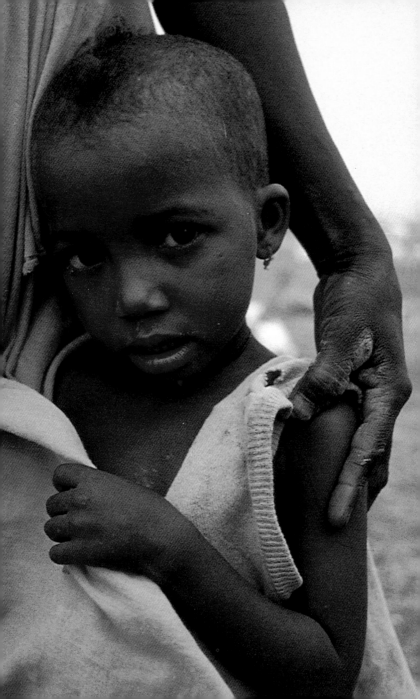

Lhasa, Tibet, 1989

Jaipur, India, 1996

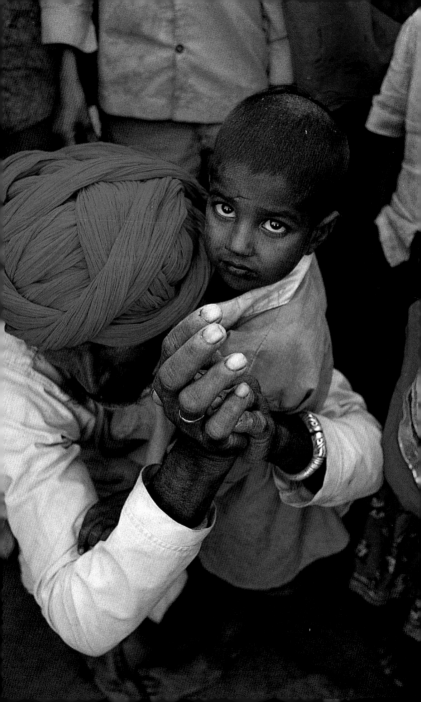

Rawalpindi, Pakistan, 1984

Feyzabad, Afghanistan, 1990

Bengal, India, 1982

West Bengal, India, 1983

Hindu Kush Mountains, Afghanistan, 1980

Manang, Nepal, 1998

Kamdesh, Afghanistan, 1980

Ghazni, Afghanistan, 1991

Al Ahmadi, Kuwait, 1991

Sikkim, India, 1998

Manang, Nepal, 1998

Rangoon, Burma, 1995

Sikkim, India, 1996

Zagreb, Croatia, 1989

Kathmandu Valley, Nepal, 1983

Timbuktu, Mali, 1986

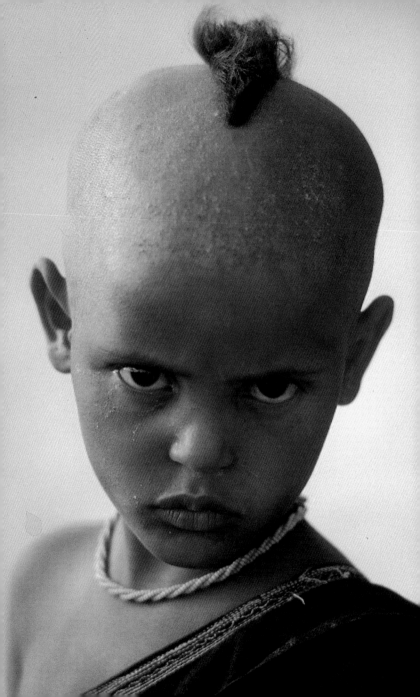

Hindu Kush mountains, Pakistan, 1980

Rangoon, Burma, 1995

Ladakh, India, 1994

Rajasthan, India, 1983

Haridwar, India, 1998

Amritsar, India, 1996

Nuwara Eliya, Sri Lanka, 1996

Shanghai, China, 1989

Filadelfia, Paraguay, 1986

Porbandar, India, 1983

Varanasi, India, 1996

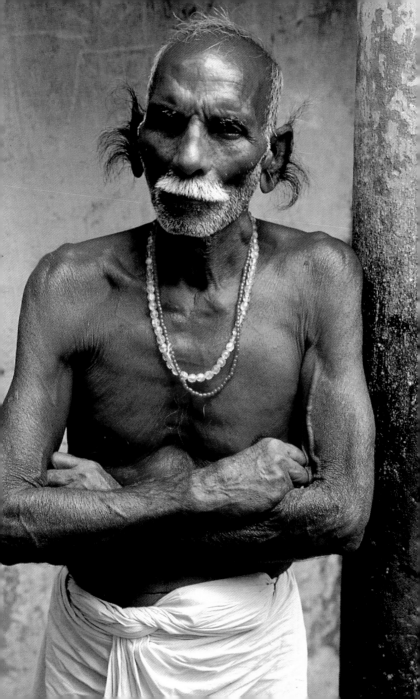

Kahan, Pakistan, 1980

Baluchistan, Pakistan, 1980

Madras, India, 1983

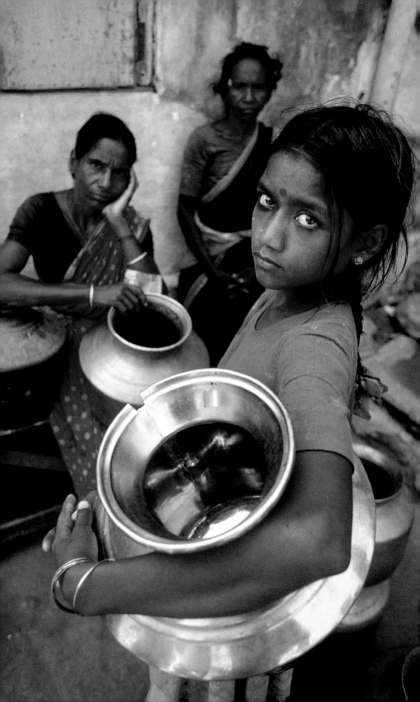

Bombay, India, 1993

Angkor Wat, Cambodia, 1986

East Germany, 1989

Haridwar, India, 1998

Landi Kotal, Pakistan, 1983

Mindanao, Philippines, 1985

Pol-e Khomri, Afghanistan, 1993

Montenegro, Yugoslavia, 1988

Phokhara, Nepal, 1984

Madhya Pradesh, India, 1996

Chaco, Paraguay, 1986

Kabul, Afghanistan, 1992

Marpha, Nepal, 1998

Tahoua, Niger, 1986

Los Angeles, USA, 1991

Luzon, Philippines, 1985

Jalalabad, Afghanistan, 1988

Kabul, Afghanistan, 1992

Kabul, Afghanistan, 1992

Luzon, Philippines, 1986

Batticaloa, Sri Lanka, 1995

Pago, Burma, 1995

Timbuktu, Mali, 1985

Phnom Penh, Cambodia, 1986

Xigaze, Tibet, 1989

Shanghai, China, 1989

Gao, Mali, 1985

Lake Chad, Chad, 1986

St. Louis, Senegal, 1985

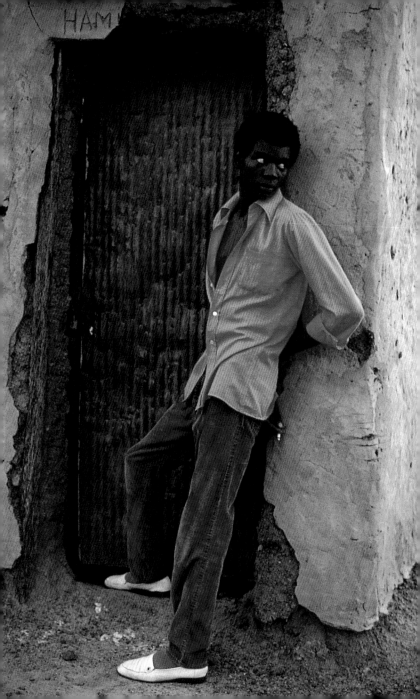

Marseilles, France, 1989

Manang, Nepal, 1998

Rangoon, Burma, 1995

Jodhpur, India, 1980

Haridwar, India, 1998

Basilan, Philippines, 1985

Lancaster, Pennsylvania, 1998

Herat, Afghanistan, 1990

West Bengal, India, 1982

Xigaze, Tibet, 1989

Kabul, Afghanistan, 1991

Jalalabad, Afghanistan, 1988

Haridwar, India, 1998

Bombay, India, 1983

Pristina, Yugoslavia, 1998

Tahoua, Niger, 1986

Mazar-e Sharif, Afghanistan, 1991

Pagan, Burma, 1995

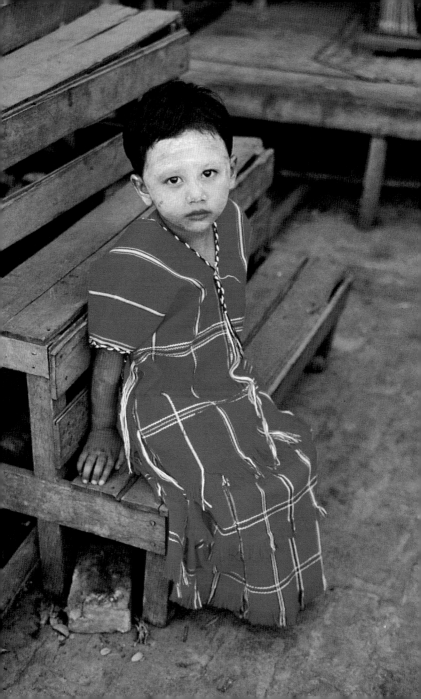

Rajasthan, India, 1997

Rome, Italy, 1996

Ajmer, Rajasthan, 1983

Los Angeles, USA, 1991

Haridwar, India, 1998

Rangoon, Burma, 1995

Mindanao, Philippines, 1985

Bombay, India, 1994

Rangoon, Burma, 1995

Chitral, Pakistan, 1980

Loikaw, Burma, 1995

NDjamena, Chad, 1985

Rangoon, Burma, 1994

Kosovo, Yugoslavia, 1989

Phnom Penh, Cambodia, 1986

Chittagong, Bangladesh, 1983

Nouakchott, Mauritania, 1985

Gujarat, India, 1996

Rangoon, Burma, 1995

Steve McCurry has photographed for *National Geographic* for 20 years
and has been a member of the Magnum photo agency since 1990.
Critically acclaimed for his colour reportage, his portrait of the
Afghan girl, featured on the cover, has become one of contemporary
photography's most celebrated and best-known portraits. Steve has
won many prizes for his photo essays shot all over the world.
He lives in New York City.

The author would like to acknowledge and thank:
Bill Allen, Chris Boot, Jo Chapman, Rich Clarkson, Bob Dannin,
Arnold Drapkin, Bruce Duffy, John Echave, David Friend, Bill Garrett,
Bob Gilka, Bill Graves, Erich Hartmann, Tom Kennedy, Kent Kobersteen,
Bill Marr, Natasha Mitchell, Danielle Oum, Kathy Ryan,
Amanda Renshaw, Elie Rogers, Richard Schlagman, Karl Shanahan,
Michele Stephenson, Robert Stevens, Amanda Tétrault and Paul Theroux

COVER: Pakistan, 1985

Phaidon Press Limited
Regent's Wharf
All Saints Street
London N1 9PA

Phaidon Press Inc.
180 Varick Street
New York
NY 10014

www.phaidon.com

First published 1999
Reprinted 1999, 2000 (twice), 2001 (twice)
© 1999 Phaidon Press Limited
Photographs © 1999 Steve McCurry

ISBN 07148 3839 X

A CIP record for this book is available from the British Library

Printed and bound in Spain